# John
# Keats

## by EDMUND BLUNDEN

Published for the British Council
and the National Book League
by Longmans, Green & Co

Edmund Blunden has for long been one of the leading authorities on the Romantic poets and writers. His books on Lamb, Leigh Hunt, Keats's publisher, and Shelley are well known, and in each of them he shows that the Romantics of English Literature are his chosen friends.

Mr Blunden's own poetry is in the lyrical vein, and he shares the special gifts of his Georgian contemporaries. His collected poems (1914–30) were followed by a second series (1930–40), *Shells by a Stream* (1944), *After the Bombing, and other Poems* (1949) and *Poems of Many Years* (1957). His last volume, *A Hong Kong House* appeared in 1966.

He was born in 1896, went to Christ's Hospital and then to Queen's College, Oxford. He served in France and Belgium from 1916 to 1919, and his *Undertones of War* (1928) is among the half dozen English books about the war which are still much read. Thereafter, he devoted himself, mainly in London, to poetry and letters with a break from 1924 to 1927 when he held the English Chair in Tokyo University. From 1931 to 1943 he was Fellow and Tutor in English at Merton College, Oxford. At the end of this time he published *Cricket Country*, in celebration of the preoccupation of a lifetime. After the war, he repeated a previous pattern by writing in London for *The Times Literary Supplement* and then revisiting Japan. A subsequent appointment was to Hong Kong. From 1966 to 1968 he was Professor of Poetry at the University of Oxford.

Mr Blunden's work is the subject of an appreciation by Mr Alec M. Hardie which appears as No. 94 in the Writers and Their Work series.

¶ JOHN KEATS was born in London in 1795, probably in October. He died in Rome on 23 February 1821, and was buried in the Protestant Cemetery, near the pyramid tomb of Caius Cestius. In the following year, Shelley's ashes were laid nearby.

JOHN KEATS

*from a painting by* WILLIAM HILTON *after a miniature by* JOSEPH SEVERN
*National Portrait Gallery*

# JOHN KEATS

by

EDMUND BLUNDEN

PUBLISHED FOR
THE BRITISH COUNCIL
AND THE NATIONAL BOOK LEAGUE
BY LONGMANS, GREEN & CO

LONGMANS, GREEN & CO LTD
Longman House, Burnt Mill, Harlow, Essex

*Associated companies, branches and
representatives throughout the world*

*First published 1950*
*Revised editions 1954, 1959, 1966*
*Reprinted with additions to Bibliography 1969*
© Edmund Blunden 1959, 1966

*Printed in Great Britain by
F. Mildner & Sons, London, EC1*

# JOHN KEATS

## I. INTRODUCTORY

For a long time it was a popular notion that Shakespeare
owed everything to a sort of wild power; that he
came into the world of literature and dominated it
without any of the received qualifications of training and
rank. The thing seemed somehow miraculous. In the
attitude of a small group of friends early in the nineteenth
century towards Shakespeare's ardent worshipper, John
Keats, a similar notion of the wonderful appears to have
played a part. That he should write poetry in spite of his
unpoetic origins, that he should write it at such an early age,
and that it should be so accomplished and glorious—these
facts amazed the acquaintances of Keats.

Perhaps that feeling towards his genius was part of the
romantic longing for 'the voice of nature' as, supposedly,
breaking through the ordinary programme of sophisticated
thought and language. That desire among lovers of literature had recently found some satisfactions. There had been
Thomas Chatterton, 'the marvellous boy', and one of
Keats's own heroes; then Robert Burns, figured as a simple
ploughman suddenly overcoming all the bards of Scotland;
and at the turn of the century Robert Bloomfield, straight
from the village green in Suffolk with his 'Farmer's Boy'.
Even while Keats was becoming known, his publishers and
others were also discovering with excitement the poetry of
John Clare, 'a Northamptonshire Peasant'. It was impossible
to line up John Keats comfortably with the series of sur-
prising 'Uneducated Poets', but admiration for him had a
touch of this in it.

His enemies in the world of letters worked upon it, and
in reviewing his poetry advised him to return without delay
to his lowly condition and proper job: 'Back to your galli-
pots'. Lord Byron, ambiguously deploring his death in *Don*

*Juan,* also discloses this feeling of something in Keats which transcended learning and study: Byron 'recorded' the strange case of this poet who

> If not intelligible, without Greek
> Contrived to talk about the Gods of late
> Much as they might have been supposed to speak.

Even now—and so it will perhaps be as long as men consider the circumstances of Keats's life—a special wonder is likely to gleam from it. But in the main the case is altered. The prevailing way of regarding Keats was indeed greatly changed in 1848, when under the editorship of Richard Monckton Milnes, afterwards Lord Houghton, two volumes of his *Life, Letters and Remains* were published. It was through that sketchy book that many readers became well aware of what subsequent biographers and better editions of the correspondence have made still clearer: Keats was not a wild genius or a 'simple soul'. His poetry, it could be seen, was akin to his intellectual range. Readers in 1848 met with the Keats, at last, who had had a good plain schooling, quickly engaged in a life of thought with unusual ability, and seriously planned his contribution to the literature of his age and country in the manner of a philosophic maturity.

In the later frame of Keats the portrait of the artist derived particularly from his Letters has had a share comparable perhaps with the poems themselves. There is no English poet, young or old, who as a character attracts and arouses younger people especially, to the same extent as he. Keats was 'ever a fighter', and even where the desire to serve him existed he would stand off according to his judgement on his own affairs. He endeavoured to keep, even at some cost, his 'own unfettered scope'. This independence was the spirit of youth, and youth to-day can read its too brief story in unaffected terms and minute detail in the Letters. Furthermore, the background to Keats's life dedicated to the revival of poetry in England is such—in his early home, in his money difficulties, in his love matters—as many living in a day of democratic expansion can readily relate to experience.

Keats's poetry, it almost needs not to be said, has continued to delight, to inform, and to meet the twentieth century. One point possibly deserves a comment here. The present era has favoured the short poem, and notably this taste has formed its preferences among the authors and performances of past centuries. Though Keats, like Shakespeare, saw the reasons for writing poems of considerable length where there was a tale to unfold, he in his turn perceived the occasions for comparative succinctness of form. And certainly he had the art of poetic distillation; in his group of odes above all he comprised in limited numbers of stanzas an abundance of feeling, fancy, suggestion, and reflection. It may be that other poets in the long roll-call who are now but seldom read were as capable in these qualities and even in the art of verse as he was; but his instinct for compactness and symmetry has left their leisurely compositions behind, while his selective richness gratifies the modern mood.

## II.  KEATS'S BOYHOOD

In 1795, perhaps on 29 or 31 October (though conjecturally in June), John Keats was born in London. He was thus seven years younger than Byron, three years younger than Shelley, of an age with Carlyle, and not so very much older than Tennyson and Dickens. Among these great writers, it is to Dickens that we turn if we look for some similarity of social position and manners to those in which Keats set forth. In 1795, the 'Reign of Terror' ended in France and Napoleon was arriving; but London life took its ordinary course. In English poetry the greatest names of the day were still Cowper and Burns.

Uncertain as we are concerning Keats's birthday—his friend Leigh Hunt says firmly 'He was a seven-months' child', which would mean a day in June 1795—we are equally unassured about the Keats ancestry. The surname is or was distributed through Southern England. Thomas Hardy was ready to believe that the poet's family tree could be traced to Dorset. The poet's father Thomas is however described by a companion of Keats as belonging further west—a native of Devon. When he comes into our view Thomas Keats has become one more Londoner, quite young, quick-witted, of good manners, and doing well. He is not however concerned with literature.

Thomas Keats was by calling a groom, and in the age of the horse his occupation was undistinguished but essential. He was in charge of the Swan and Hoop livery stables—where you might take your horse to be looked after, or hire a horse for your occasion—on Finsbury Pavement, convenient to the offices of London City men. The proprietor of the stables, John Jennings, made a fortune, which to-day might be equivalent to £50,000 or more. His daughter Frances married his manager, Thomas Keats, in 1794. Their home was first at the sign of the Swan and Hoop.

The children of Thomas and Frances Keats—described as 'a lively woman'—were five in number, so far as records tell. The first-born was named John. Two other boys grew up, George (born in 1797) and Tom (born in 1799). John was to die in Italy, George in America. A daughter, Frances Mary (born in 1803), outlived all the sons, married a Spanish gentleman named Llanos, and is buried in Madrid.

Several occurrences in the childhood of John Keats were unpropitious; and one was the sudden death of his father, flung from his horse as he was riding home one night in April 1804. With hardly any delay Keats's mother married William Rawlings, a business man, who seems thus to have transferred the Swan and Hoop stables to his own property.

This marriage—it is believed—was a failure. At any rate the children of Thomas Keats were taken to live with Mrs Jennings, their grandmother, at Edmonton, then a village north of London. Old Mr Jennings, their grandfather, died in March 1805. Their mother drifted. At last she returned to the home at Edmonton, where she died in 1810; thereupon her children's affairs were legally handed over to certain guardians. Mrs Jennings, an excellent grandmother, to whose virtues one or two of John Keats's poems pay tribute, died in December 1814.

These vicissitudes speak for themselves. But children do not generally continue conscious of great afflictions; the Keats children enjoyed domestic comfort and indulgence enough to forget them. The prosperity of Mr Jennings had assured them of almost everything they wanted. Their home was one of a good many in early nineteenth-century London which the caricatures of George Cruikshank (a contemporary of Keats) illustrate for us in great detail. Furniture and food were profuse. Gold sovereigns, or guineas, were not too hard to find when bills were presented. As for the intellectual and artistic side of life, we cannot feel so sure; but we know one thing.

Frances Keats had a wish, or an ambition, to send her boys to Harrow School, not far away, which was already illustrious. It was also expensive. But two of her brothers had been happy at a much smaller and humbler school, and to that school it was decided to send John, George, and subsequently Tom Keats.

The school has long disappeared. The coming of the railway demanded its site. Yet it lived in fame, chiefly because John Keats attended there. It was founded in 1786, in a fine old Georgian country house at Enfield, with the gardens, meadows, and outbuildings usual to such strongholds of retired merchants. No modern school could be more pleasantly circumstanced. There were seventy or eighty pupils. The master was a kind and sensible man named John Clarke. He kept an eye not only on the school but on current literature, science, and politics, and regarded education as an exercise in reasonable liberty. Mrs Clarke in girlhood had written poems.

From about 1803 to 1810, or 1811—the usual period of secondary education in that age—John Keats was a boarder at Mr Clarke's school.

Before investigating what he learned there we should resume a matter already introduced—something which was a force in the life of Keats until the end. Under the will of his grandfather John Jennings, augmented by Mrs Jennings in a deed, Keats with his brothers and his sister was technically made secure from poverty. Children as they were, they did not bother their heads with the exact terms of the transaction. They came to know, at least, that one of their two guardians, Mr Richard Abbey, was a mighty figure in their lives. The other disappeared.

Abbey came from Yorkshire—from the very village where Mrs Jennings had passed her childhood. In London he had become a tea-merchant. He was an ordinary city wholesaler, made a safe income, supported the dignity of commerce, and gave both time and cheques to charities. Inevitably Abbey agreed with the existing order of things. When the disconcerting John Keats was placed under his control, it was one of life's little ironies. To Keats it was not a little one, but that will appear as we go on.

At Enfield Keats learned the usual history, geography, sums, grammar, some Latin and French, and the rest; the time came when he discovered the resources of the school library. But it was not as a scholar that he first impressed the other boys. He was renowned instead as a fighter, always ready to use his fists, and as a champion 'in all active exercises'. His appearance was strikingly beautiful. His passionate temper was matched by his uproarious love of the grotesque and comical. A sailor uncle (on the Jennings' side of the family) was his idol, and it seemed that John Keats might become eminent 'in some military capacity'.

But at that period a strong new influence in Mr Clarke's

school was taking the clever boys away from such careers. Edward Cowper, to name one of Keats's schoolfellows, became an inventor whose share in improving printing machines is part of the history of *The Times* newspaper. Another, Edward Holmes, organist and music critic, is duly remembered as the author of the first real English biography of Mozart. The fresh influence which probably worked in them at Enfield was the enlightened, energetic, and benevolent personality of the assistant master, Charles Cowden Clarke, John's son. He was only sixteen years old when Keats entered the school.

To that young teacher Keats wrote later on,

> Ah! had I never seen,
> Or known your kindness, what might I have been?

Cowden Clarke was always—but this was true of him in all known instances—affectionate and admiring towards the boy; yet it was when Keats's time for leaving school was drawing near that he really devoted himself to bringing him out. Then, in his fourteenth and fifteenth years, Keats lost his appetite for 'manly sports' and disclosed his passion for looking into all sorts of books and winning all possible school prizes. He even wrote out his prose renderings of Virgil's long poem, the *Aeneid*. Keats was now charmed by the classical mythology of gods and heroes wherever he could find it—in drowsy dictionaries or in the visions of the poets.

In February 1810 the death of Keats's mother led to his coming under the authority of Mr Abbey, and perhaps at the end of the year that guardian apprenticed him to a surgeon named Hammond at Edmonton. Why this choice of a profession was made, except that it was highly respected and comparatively profitable, nobody can say; Keats may have thought of it himself as one in which his Latin would be practical; probably it was simply that the opportunity arose at the right moment, and so near his grandmother's house.

## III.  DISCOVERING POETRY

At Hammond's the work does not seem to have been heavy, and Keats was able to walk over to his old school and talk with Cowden Clarke many a sunny hour. There was an arbour in the garden which was the very place for sitting and consulting. Clarke lent the boy books and awakened his tastes as before. Through him Keats became a 'constant reader' of *The Examiner*, a weekly paper in which reforms of various kinds were recommended with slashing brilliance and courage. Through Clarke again, who played the piano, Keats began to enjoy Mozart. At length Keats requested the loan of Edmund Spenser's great book *The Faerie Queene*.

This request puzzled Clarke a little, and even more it amused old Mr and Mrs Clarke, whose admiration for Keats had not included the notion that he would ever turn poetical. But it soon appeared that *The Faerie Queene* was exactly what Keats wanted, and his friend was delighted to observe his abounding enjoyment of the poem. Their talks grew increasingly eager on poetic pleasures, and the schoolmaster explained the different sorts of metre and of form, and commented on some living poets of the age.

In 1815 Keats became a medical student in London, attending lectures at Guy's Hospital and progressing well enough to be given the certificate—in the summer of 1816—authorizing him to practise as an apothecary. His fellow-students however were quickly sure that poetry was his dominant study, and his brothers already told everybody that John was destined for greatness. Mr Abbey rather destined him for a surgeon's practice at Tottenham, but when he opened this proposition to Keats it was declined. 'I do not intend to be a Surgeon.' 'Not intend to be a Surgeon! Why, what do you mean to be?' 'I mean to rely upon my abilities as a poet.'

This conversation (Abbey never forgot it) occurred probably at the end of 1816, by which time Keats had written a good deal of poetry. He made his first attempt in 1813, it seems, calling it 'Imitation of Spenser'. His early verses, as is natural, were partly imitations of various poets, some of them contemporary with him. Even the 'Imitation of Spenser', a pretty fragment which as we have it must surely have been carefully revised between 1813 and 1816, recalls eighteenth-century Spenserians rather than the sumptuous original.

The tracing out of the relationship of Keats's juvenilia to other compositions is not to be tried here, except in respect of Cowden Clarke's tuition. Clarke was one of those who saw in Leigh Hunt, the editor of *The Examiner*, a champion of liberty not only in politics but in poetics also—not only as a critic, moreover, but as a poet still young. Hunt was full of ardour for a new way in English poetry, and called for a revolt against the 'correct' school in metre, phrase and matter. Let us have, he said, a return to nature, a vivacity of feeling and a luxuriance of fancy. Clarke expected Hunt's triumph. Keats caught the excitement.

In a poem actually entitled 'Politics and Poetics' (1811) collected by Hunt in this book *The Feast of the Poets* (1815) there were such yearnings as this:

> Oh, for a seat in some poetic nook,
> Just hid with trees, and sparkling with a brook,
> Where through the quivering boughs the sunbeams shoot
> Their airy diamonds upon flower and fruit,
> While stealing airs come fuming o'er the stream;

and such scenery and such visions of the spirits of nature as followed accorded with the poetical rambles of Clarke and Keats round Enfield. Hunt went much further in 'fancy and familiarity' before long, as well as in an experimental versification, until in 1816 he published his much praised and much reviled *Story of Rimini*.

If, as historians of the poetic education of Keats, we examine the dates of some of Hunt's pieces as printed by him, especially in his newspaper, we find some curious surprises. His dashing and garrulous 'Epistle to Lord

Byron' might be supposed to have given the note for Keats's manner in epistolary poems,[1] but Keats's 'Epistle to George Felton Mathew' was written in November 1815 and Hunt addressed Byron in *The Examiner* of 28 April 1816. Certainly a number of sonnets by Hunt will have been admired by Keats in that journal at a date when they might kindle his desire to write sonnets himself. On the whole, it is enough to regard *The Examiner's* poetry and theories, especially with Clarke's resonant comments, as stimulating Keats's advance into his own poetical regions. To blame Hunt for all the weaknesses and freaks in Keats's early work, or to applaud him for all the colour and fragrance there, is theorizing of small importance.

Though Keats's early verses are devoted to pleasant things and admirations, and their most marked character is the scattered multitude of beautiful observations from nature in happy moods, they are not limited to these.

> The clouds were pure and white as flocks new shorn,
> And fresh from the clear brook; sweetly they slept
> On the blue fields of heaven, and then there crept
> A little noiseless noise among the leaves,
> Born of the very sigh that silence heaves. . . .
> So I straightway began to pluck a posey
> Of luxuries bright, milky, soft and rosy. . . .

That indeed is the young Keats—in 1816—but he shows another side of his virility in the sonnet, for example, 'written on the day that Mr Leigh Hunt left prison'. The day was 3 February 1815, and Hunt had been serving a sentence of two years in gaol for an adjudged political libel (an attack on the Prince Regent). Keats writes so vehemently that one might almost think he was trying to get himself into the same sort of trouble.

Although, apart from Clarke, Keats had the company of

[1] Those who read older English poetry, that of Elizabethans like Drayton and Ben Jonson, or of seventeenth-century John Dryden—and these were being recommended by Hunt and others when Keats was a youth—will recognize the 'Epistolary' style as a much earlier tradition.

one or two versifiers of about his own age, it was not until he met Leigh Hunt that his literary life opened out. 'Twill be an era in my existence', he declared concerning Clarke's introducing him to Hunt, and he was not wrong. The meeting happened probably in mid-October 1816 at Hunt's cottage in the Vale of Health, Hampstead, at that time the resort of quite a host of literary, artistic, musical, and political celebrities. Hunt had already found a place in *The Examiner* for a sonnet on 'Solitude' by Keats and had read some of his other pieces. The recognition of blossoming genius which was Hunt's ('The Indicator's') gift did not fail here. Moreover he instantly took a great liking to Keats, who became a welcome guest at the crowded cottage on the Heath whenever he cared to come.

There at once Keats had a new circle of interesting acquaintances. Now he could talk with William Hazlitt, painter and impassioned critic; with B. R. Haydon, to whose studio and all the vast imaginative designs in development there he was soon invited; with P. B. Shelley, a Sussex gentleman of vegetarian principles who had circulated a heretical poem called *Queen Mab*; with J. H. Reynolds, a witty young city clerk whose verses had pleased Lord Byron; with Vincent Novello the organist and editor of great music—and still many others.

But for a time Hunt himself, a man of thirty-two, 'matchless as a fireside companion', was Keats's paragon. Hunt's readers in the weekly paper were soon given a surprise and a prophecy in an article 'Young Poets'— 1 December 1816—pointing out two newcomers of the highest promise, Shelley and Keats, with a possible third, Reynolds. Hunt was able to quote one sonnet by Keats, of recent date, which instantly justified him; it stands to this day among Keats's noblest and best constructed poems; it was 'On First Looking into Chapman's Homer'. The particular copy of that Elizabethan translation had been lent to Clarke by one of Hunt's friends, Mr Alsager of *The Times*.

In a longer poem called 'Sleep and Poetry' written about the end of 1816 Keats records with a passion and a vision his state of mind now that the highway to Parnassus appeared to be unbarred for him. He counted over a great many of the bright and pleasurable images out of which his fancy would make festivals; but he thought also of 'the events of this wide world' and of his passing on to 'the agonies, the strife of human hearts'. Keats gave his help, too, to Leigh Hunt's policy of denouncing and cauterizing the 'French school of poetry', which in England meant the followers of Alexander Pope. Among the lines which described his own notion of poetry some quickly became well known:

> A drainless shower
> Of light is poesy; 'tis the supreme of power;
> 'Tis might half slumbering on its own right arm.

During those winter months, living with his brothers in busy Cheapside but often passing an evening with Hunt, Keats revised old poems and composed new, and was urged to appear with a volume. Two friends of Hunt, Charles and James Ollier—remembered best as Shelley's publishers—had lately set up their business, and they accepted Keats's book. At the last moment a dedication was called for. The author, quitting the party at which the message was delivered, wrote that dedication in the form of a sonnet addressed to Leigh Hunt. Since the sheets contained a poem of gratitude to Cowden Clarke for earlier ministrations, this was impartial justice. In March 1817 *Poems, by John Keats*, one of hundreds of small volumes of verse in that decade, was on sale. Not many buyers came forward, not many reviewers took the opportunity; but Leigh Hunt in *The Examiner* wrote at great length on the true nature of poetry and the renaissance of English poetry signified by this new book.

Out of the poems in Keats's first book—not at all a bulky volume—one sonnet shall be given here, both as a glimpse of Keats as he was in the year 1816, with all his new world opening to his warm imagination, and as already a well-made sonnet with sympathy, thought, imagery, and realism contained in a balanced deployment. *Not to flashy, dry Imagery — kind o s to the point*

> Keen, fitful gusts are whisp'ring here and there
>> Among the bushes half leafless, and dry;
>> The stars look very cold about the sky,
> And I have many miles on foot to fare.
> Yet feel I little of the cool bleak air,
>> Or of the dead leaves rustling drearily,
>> Or of those silver lamps that burn on high,
> Or of the distance from home's pleasant lair;
> For I am brimfull of the friendliness
>> That in a little cottage I have found;
> Of fair-hair'd Milton's eloquent distress,
>> And all his love for gentle Lycid drown'd;
> Of lovely Laura in her light green dress,
>> And faithful Petrarch gloriously crown'd.

## IV. THE POET IN HIS CAREER

Had John Keats not met Leigh Hunt in his early days, no doubt he would have entered the literary world through some other enthusiast's introductions; it might have taken him rather longer to do so. The advantages which Hunt's personality and position in the world of letters and journalism gave him, as yet unknown and uncertain of himself, are evident. He was named in an Almanack in 1817 as a celebrity. There were serious disadvantages, and Keats was soon able to see them, partly from his own judgement and partly from the instruction of others.

It was a mixed blessing in 1817 to be the subject of *Examiner* encomiums. *The Examiner* was the refreshment of many a reader north and south, Sunday by Sunday, but it was looked on as poison by many more, for it existed as an instrument of a party determined to change the old order. Leigh Hunt was a notorious enemy of the conservatives. His known associates therefore received from their journalists all the punishment which was being given to him principally because of his political opinions, and in a degree for his literary insubordination. Politics and poetics were assailed together, and 'inside information' (anything would do) concerning private life was joyfully worked upon.

But Keats had other difficulties—or disturbances—as one of Hunt's circle. These appeared quickly enough. He did not feel at home with people of Shelley's rank, or Shelley's way of thinking—and Shelley, who had advised him not to publish his book, though he had published some by himself, was Hunt's real Immortal. Haydon, the painter, effusive in his adoration of Keats, was turning away from his old friend Hunt after drab quarrels on points of religious orthodoxy. Reynolds—not the painter—was all for Keats, but was bored with Hunt. In short, the Hunt party looked like breaking up—not altogether, but through such weakenings. Let us add that Messrs Ollier did not propose to publish for Keats again, his first volume having failed in the trade.

That failure could not blind true judges of poetry to the imaginative, pictorial and sensuous beauties in the book, and in a short time Keats, through the introduction of John Reynolds, was welcomed by another rising publishing firm. John Taylor and James Hessey, of 93 Fleet Street, were now prosperous enough through their sales of useful and moral works to increase the literary side of their business, and they were poetical enough to perceive in young Keats a star of the age. They quickly agreed to publish, when he should have written it, a long new poem, a narrative poem which, considering the numerous recent publications of the sort and their fame, might be really popular. Taylor and Hessey advanced him money enough to secure favourable circumstances for the months to be spent in the toil of composition.

The subject Keats chose was one which he had already touched on, from Greek mythology—that of Endymion, fabled to have loved the Moon. He treated it very freely and discursively, to the indignation of strict classical scholars like T. L. Peacock, who sometimes came to Leigh Hunt's house. Keats's tale of wonder, originally of simple outline, grew complicated in his hands. He began with the lines,

> A thing of beauty is a joy for ever:
> Its loveliness increases; it will never
> Pass into nothingness;

and he proceeded almost regardless whither, so long as things of beauty might be multiplied,

> And now at once, adventuresome, I send
> My herald thought into a wilderness:
> There let its trumpet blow, and quickly dress
> My uncertain path with green, that I may speed
> Easily onward, through flowers and weed.

Keats spent periods in 1817 away from London, in order that he might write *Endymion* with his unconfirmed and undistracted powers; he stayed in the Isle of Wight, at Margate, at Oxford, and when he set down the last line he was at Burford Bridge, in Surrey. But even in London he now gained something like pastoral surroundings for the creation of his pastoral poem, settling with his brothers that summer at Hampstead.

His visit to Oxford was in the main exceedingly happy and congenial. Reynolds had introduced him to a poet (in manuscript) named Benjamin Bailey, a student at a decaying institution called Magdalen Hall; and there, to enjoy Oxford in the vacation, Keats stayed as Bailey's guest through September. While Bailey (a clergyman in the making) read his books, Keats at another table in the room wrote his daily portion of Book III of *Endymion*. Their labours were varied with tours and wanderings, such as Oxford still provides so well, in the city and round it, and with boating explorations on the Cherwell and the Isis. Bailey was enchanted with his companion's appearance ('the youthful Apollo'), his manly yet gentle character, and easy conversation. Much of it turned on literature, the art of poetry, and favourite passages; and it is notable that by this date Keats had become an admirer though not a wholesale panegyrist of Wordsworth.

Keats was gathering new friends, all with a zest for poetry, at speed. The list includes Charles Brown, an odd creature, brought up in commerce, something of a writer and an artist, and Charles Wentworth Dilke, a civil servant who had been publishing a collection of old plays—his bigger achievement as editor of *The Athenaeum* was to come too late for Keats to support it. Brown and Dilke had built in 1815 and 1816 a graceful and roomy house at Hampstead called Wentworth Place, which soon had a special and central eminence in the history of Keats.

Perhaps Keats had met Joseph Severn, a young painter, some time earlier; James Rice, a solicitor and a writer of trifles in verse, an excellent friend, came to him as the companion of J. H. Reynolds; and Richard Woodhouse, another lawyer, was one of Taylor and Hessey's intimates and advisers. Woodhouse, a schoolfellow but decrier of Shelley, was a tireless scholar of European poetry, and he conceived so great a zeal for the newly discovered Keats as to constitute himself the unofficial editor of everything from Keats's pen that he could get. With remarkable precision Woodhouse compiled, compared, commented on all the manuscripts; and though he did not himself publish his collections they were to emerge as a priceless benefaction to later editors and biographers.

In general during the year 1817 Keats was in a company where literary principles and methods and the intellect of the age were freely discussed. But besides, his taste for the fine arts had proper play alike in symposia and in observation of statues, pictures, architecture, and even gems and cameos. He took his time among the Elgin Marbles at the British Museum, of which Haydon was so tremendous an advocate; he became so much of a connoisseur in painting as to 'discover' at Oxford a young artist for himself, Charles Cripps. In the days of the Prince Regent the fine arts alike in private and in public were quite in favour, and Keats was of his period; but it was of profound importance to him, the most aesthetic of the young poets, to be more and more intimate with them. Similarly, his classic imagination being considered, the new resources of imagery from the ancient world were invaluable.

His school nevertheless was often that of nature and the months, and he studied these on the seashore and in woody landscapes day and night. In this way he enriched his long poem, which he completed at Burford Bridge—as was mentioned—on 28 October 1817. But, as H. W. Garrod pointed out, he went on with drastic revisions, as one who could not come to an end of his poetic treasures, even after his *Endymion* had been set up in type by Taylor and Hessey's printer.

In December 1817 Wordsworth was in London, and Keats, who had already said in an irritable moment that he was disgusted with literary men and would never know another except Wordsworth, was able to see something of him, and even to read the 'Hymn to Pan' out of *Endymion* to him. Wordsworth was already aware of Keats the poet, but he did not respond as joyfully as Keats hoped; his dignity and punctilious attention to the forms of society overhung their meetings; and once more Keats was 'disgusted' with literary men. 'I will have no more of Wordsworth or Hunt in particular', he wrote.

But Keats was very young and wildly impulsive. Wordsworth seems to have known more of his track than he imagined; for the Lake Poet was to describe him as 'too good for the sorry company that he keeps', alluding apparently to the sporting life which Reynolds and others tried to live. The depth to which Wordsworth's poetry had become familiar to and accepted by Keats may be seen by comparisons of their works. As for Hunt, a bond of some kind existed, strong enough for Keats to be with him for the accustomed evenings of fancy, food, music, and verse competitions. One of these (4 February 1918) gave us three finely imaginative sonnets on the Nile by Keats,

Shelley, and Hunt. It was not quite the last time that Keats and Shelley met, but Shelley left England in March; and the simplest comments on his attitude towards Keats is that he included Keats among the eight writers to whom his publishers were instructed to send presentation copies of all his works.

In March 1818 Keats left London. His brother Tom was at Teignmouth in Devonshire, a consumptive under the care of Dr Turton. At Teignmouth it seemed possible that John, who stayed until May, might fall in love with one of the daughters of Mrs Jeffrey. He had from time to time admired one girl or another. Marian Jeffrey however was to marry Mr Prowse; what is curious is that she then published a book of her own poems, and that her son William Jeffrey Prowse (originally 'announced' by Leigh Hunt's eldest son) was a delightful writer of humorous verse.

Tom Keats survived only until 7 December 1818. He had been taken back to Hampstead by John, who thereafter nursed him with the fondest devotion—at least, once Tom's illness had become such as to need incessant attention. George Keats was not there to give it; he married Georgiana Wylie and emigrated to America in June 1818. Some of the circle believed that in order to keep going there George drew heavily on John's funds and left him much embarrassed; it has not been proved. But the community of interests of the three brothers was shattered in 1818, and John, no longer the strong and healthy youth of Cowden Clarke's recollection, was left to make a home in London for himself.

## V. 'O EARLY LOST!'

Much trouble was taken to send *Endymion: a Poetic Romance* into the world with an appropriate Preface, and Keats, observant of his friends' advice, succeeded in writing one; perhaps, however, the tone of admitting his own dissatisfaction with the work which he was publishing was injudicious. Now, that admission is entirely honourable to Keats as man and poet; then, it was merely an invitation to the malicious—something that the enemies of Leigh Hunt and his comrades were enraptured to read.

The poem appeared in April 1818, and Leigh Hunt's *Foliage* with a sonnet to Keats in it and numerous similarities of allusion, verse, and vocabulary was out at about the same time. It was almost too easy for the haters of the Reformists to fire away at Keats as one of Hunt's niminy-piminy set of upstarts, including Hazlitt and Haydon, termed 'The Cockney School'. The jocular rogues of *Blackwood's* in Edinburgh had informers in London and could make their attacks on Keats damnably personal. But the worst blow was dealt by the *Quarterly Review*, for that was in every reading-room and was credited with almost divine authority.

Opinions differ over the effect of the *Quarterly's* article (September 1818) on Keats; we know what Shelley heard, and what in 'Adonais' presently he purposed to avenge— that the effect was deadly. In a sense, it was; for Keats had hoped that his poem, being after all a romance—what were Scott's poems, and Byron's?—would bring in some money to his need. That straightforward hope was dashed, no matter how many friendly reviews of *Endymion* moderated the pain of rejection; the *Quarterly* had done what its queer little editor, Gifford, had said it should, and stopped the sale. A writer who had presumed to denounce the tradition of Pope and 'correctness' in our national poetry could not be permitted to live.

In the summer following the publication of *Endymion* Keats went with his brother George to Liverpool, and after seeing George's ship leave he continued northwards in the company of Charles Brown. They were going on the old-fashioned 'picturesque tour' through the Lakes into Scotland. Wordsworth once again disappointed—he was away as an election agent when they called at his house. And he was on the opposite side in politics. However the mountains were at home; Keats 'beheld them with an epic eye'. They wandered through the country of Robert Burns, and even got over to Ireland between seeing where he died and where he was born. They passed further, they climbed Ben Nevis—but Keats was unwell, and while Brown tramped on he perforce returned aboard a coaster to London. There he was confronted with the last illness of 'poor Tom'.

Upon Tom's death Keats moved into Brown's house, Wentworth Place, where he could read and write in comfort. But through this removal he entered upon the greatest of all his agitations: he had long been 'half in love', and now he felt it all. A widow, Mrs Brawne, who had rented the house during the Scotch tour, had a daughter named Fanny, 'a young thing', elegant, exotic, coy. Keats saw her flirting and in his own style quietly resolved to carry her off. But this was not a simple matter; Miss Brawne was not so sure, and even when he had more or less persuaded her that they were meant for one another she held to her liberty. With this mingled rapture and misery Keats was to pass the rest of his life.

During 1818 Keats made many and lasting additions to his poetical works, one of them originally intended to be published in a volume shared by him and Reynolds. The two poets were to offer some of Boccaccio's stories in English metres. 'Isabella, or, the Pot of Basil' was all that Keats produced, but it was beautiful. The writer was ascertaining how to proportion his richness of epithet, comparison, and mellifluous language to the feelings, the idea, and progress of the whole narrative. A kind of companion-piece was begun about the end of the year, 'The Eve of St Agnes', and early in 1819 another, left incomplete, 'The Eve of St Mark'. In these Keats's imaginations turned not to Italy but to the 'old England' of which so many peaceful and gracious vestiges were easily found in his travels, and which had been depicted latterly by men like S. T. Coleridge and Walter Scott. In both poems he achieved legendary beauty, with something (especially in the second) of the fantastic and supernatural. In 'Lamia' he used a Greek tale, with a moral which enabled him to play on those stops most brilliantly.

For painting in verse, most of 'The Eve of St Mark' has peculiar precision and at the same time ease and grace of composition, with pure clean colours; it was apparently to be a simple story in the incidents, and so Keats gave even greater attention than usual to the setting. In general, that setting is an ancient English cathedral city (and Keats knew more than one), but the picture-writing comes to its height in the 'interior' when the poet sets his heroine Bertha down in her room to read her book of the saints by firelight:

> All was silent, all was gloom,
> Abroad and in the homely room:
> Down she sat, poor cheated soul!
> And struck a lamp from the dismal coal;
> Leaned forward, with bright drooping hair
> And slant book, full against the glare.
> Her shadow, in uneasy guise,
> Hover'd about, a giant size,
> On ceiling-beam and old oak chair,
> The parrot's cage, and panel square;
> And the warm angled winter screen,
> On which were many monsters seen,
> Call'd doves of Siam, Lima mice,
> And legless birds of Paradise,
> Macaw and tender Av'davat,
> And silken-furr'd Angora cat.
> Untired she read, her shadow still
> Glower'd about, as it would fill
> The room with wildest forms and shades,
> As though some ghostly queen of spades
> Had come to mock behind her back,
> And dance, and ruffle her garments black.

Other attempts in other styles dated 1818 decidedly prove his variety. He only finished the first movement of an Ode to May, but it has serene strength and promises 'great verse'. Some 'Extracts from an Opera' tantalize us; where is the rest? That opera would have been bright and beautiful, if the music had matched the lyrics. But before the year was out Keats was applying all his poetic gifts to a poem on a classical myth, *Hyperion*, which if he could sustain it would illustrate poesy and endeavour with his profoundest ideas on them. Giant forms of fable appeared to his inward eye, and he expressed the pageant in his sublimest style. The work went on into the spring of 1819.

To complete the story: Keats—and this again exhibits his scope as a poet—came to dislike his grand exercise, and put it from him. He began afresh, in a more auto-biographical and reflective mood, calling his new version *The Fall of Hyperion—A Dream*. Once again, the search for an answer to the question, 'What is poetry?' was uppermost in him. But the new version also remained a fragment. The old one haunted it and harassed him.

In 1819, despite Brown's kindness, Keats was not perfectly settled at Wentworth Place. Like his brother, he had thoughts of going abroad. He spoke of South America. He thought he might get there as a ship's doctor. Brown thought it would be enough to go out of London now and then. One welcome 'furlough' was that at Winchester, from August to October. It was part of Keats's problem that half of Wentworth Place was now taken by Mrs Brawne and her family. Another thing was that he needed an income, beyond his remains of legacies and rents. Journalism might bring it; he would try. Dilke found him lodgings in Westminster, and he went there after Winchester—but he found himself alone. In a few days he was back at Hampstead. Fanny was there—and she received him lovingly.

When could he offer her marriage? His ship would not come home. Brown was always trying to help. A popular play? They had written one together, *Otho the Great*, but it did not yet bring them the right letter from a manager. It never has. Brown, a character who liked a joke, suggested a comic fairy tale—the period had had a few. Keats was full of waggery himself, and went ahead with *The Cap and Bells*, which had no discernible plot—but the author muttered doggedly that all would come right in the end. The end was never reached, nor the visionary royalties. In this dubious state of affairs the year 1819 closed for John Keats.

But he had written that year a group of poems which in many opinions place him on a level with the greatest artists in all the kinds of expression. Keats's odes alone would uphold his fame and his character if every other scrap by and about him were lost. The ode in England had followed, more or less, two models; and Keats, unlike Shelley, preferred the Roman ode to the Greek when he saw that his occasion required less than an epic and more than a sonnet. He learned from Spenser; and perhaps from William Collins, the eighteenth-century author of an Ode to Simplicity and another to Evening.

It is immaterial here to be chronological on Keats's group of odes, which are on the following subjects: To Psyche, A Nightingale, A Grecian Urn, Autumn, Indolence, Melancholy (and one to Fanny). Two of these, the 'Nightingale' in July 1819 and the 'Grecian Urn' in December, appeared in a magazine entitled *Annals of the Fine Arts*, signed merely †. Another celebrated poem by Keats written in 1819 seems to be a delayed expression of his journey through the region of Scottish Border minstrelsy, as well as an allegory of his life—namely, 'La Belle Dame Sans Merci'.

So great was the worship of the long poem in Keats's day that even critics like Lamb and Shelley scarcely perceived the calm glory of such odes by Keats as they read; Lamb was for basing his future name on the narrative poems, and Shelley on the fragmentary epic *Hyperion*. But they cannot have failed to see the delightful dreaming in which the odes excel: or the manner in which the poet returns from the dream to the actual. That moving sequence of reverie and reality is in the 'Ode to a Nightingale':

> Thou wast not born for death, immortal Bird!
>     No hungry generations tread thee down;
> The voice I hear this passing night was heard
>     In ancient days by emperor and clown:
> Perhaps the self-same song that found a path
>     Through the sad heart of Ruth, when, sick for home,
>         She stood in tears amid the alien corn;
>             The same that oft-times hath
>         Charm'd magic casements, opening on the foam
>             Of perilous seas, in faery lands forlorn.
>
> Forlorn! the very word is like a bell
>     To toll me back from thee to my sole self!
> Adieu! the fancy cannot cheat so well
>     As she is fam'd to do, deceiving elf.

Again in the 'Grecian Urn':

> Who are these coming to the sacrifice?
>     To what green altar, O mysterious priest,
> Lead'st thou that heifer lowing at the skies,
>     And all her silken flanks with garlands drest?
> What little town by river or sea shore,
>     Or mountain-built with peaceful citadel,
>         Is emptied of this folk, this pious morn?
> And, little town, thy streets for evermore
>     Will silent be; and not a soul to tell
>         Why thou art desolate, can e'er return.
>
> O Attic shape! Fair attitude! with brede
>     Of marble men and maidens overwrought,
> With forest branches and the trodden weed;
>     Thou, silent form, dost tease us out of thought
> As doth eternity: Cold Pastoral!
>     When old age shall this generation waste,
>         Thou shalt remain, in midst of other woe
> Than ours, a friend to men, to whom thou say'st,
>     Beauty is truth, truth beauty,—that is all
>         Ye know on earth, and all ye need to know.

Soon after the opening of 1820 the ominous gloom of

that ballad, 'La Belle Dame', became more intelligible; Keats fell into what was called 'a decline'. He was ordered to bed, and kept there through February and most of March. He appeared to recover, and made a trip or two to town, but with a mind far from quiet, for he feared that Fanny was playing with him. In May he moved into lodgings at Kentish Town, not far from Leigh Hunt's home at that date; and very soon the Hunts persuaded him to become their guest. He remained there and they nursed him until 12 August, when an unlucky incident over a delayed letter from Fanny—he afterwards saw it all better in his natural temper—upset him, and off he went to Hampstead. Mrs Brawne then took care of him.

It had been arranged meanwhile that his third book should be published—a gathering of the poems since *Endymion*, mentioned above, and some others. The editorial work of course fell principally upon Taylor and Woodhouse, though Keats might visit the publishing office or otherwise do a little about the volume. *Lamia, Isabella*, &c. was published early in July 1820, and the notices were numerous and favourable; Leigh Hunt and Charles Lamb wrote two of the best of them. The demand for the book was not furious but it was encouraging; it could however hardly encourage Keats, who had been medically advised by leading physicians that his only chance of survival lay in his going to Italy. He had fallen out with Mr Abbey, so that his application for a loan was useless; and his ignorance of his own affairs excluded him from what still lingered of his own funds in the Court of Chancery. Taylor and Hessey got up a subscription list, with the aid of Taylor's brother James, a banker, so that at least he might travel to Italy and try his luck. But who could and would accompany him?

That question was easier to settle than it looked. Joseph Severn, the artist, had won from the Royal Academy the option of going to Italy as a student. He was asked to make his way there with Keats and although his father knocked him down for his 'folly' he said he would go. On 18 September 1821 the *Maria Crowther*, a small brig, sailed with the painter and poet among the passengers; the weather in the Channel was such that they were given chances to land now and again on English soil, and Keats even visited old friends near Portsmouth. But at last— Italy; first Naples, then Rome, and in Rome (thanks to Taylor) Keats was befriended by Dr James Clark. Lodgings at No. 26 Piazza di Spagna were 'according to plan'.

On board ship and for some time in Italy Keats had done his best to figure as a robust and spirited young traveller, but it was heroic acting; and at Rome the conventional treatment of consumption in which Dr Clark trusted soon ended it. The whole story (for Severn wrote in great detail of it) must be read elsewhere. Poetry, it is clear, had yielded to illness and anxiety long before, and the last scene is that of a man in love doomed to death; Keats did not open Fanny's letters. He died on the night of 23 February 1821; early on 26 February he was buried in the Protestant Cemetery near the pyramid tomb of Caius Cestius, a proximity which is duly considered in a poem by Keats's admirer, Thomas Hardy.

## VI.   CONCLUSION

For generations the poems of Keats have been enjoyed, imitated and venerated. The calumnies and the contempt of those who once decried him did not in fact prevent some of his excellent inspirations from finding their way quite soon to the ordinary reader, even if they got there in some book on natural history or a sketch of modern literature. And that was long ago. For many years, the discovery of any unpublished poem by Keats has been regarded as a national event (see, for instance, *The Times* of 14 April 1914). It is regrettable that such discoveries can hardly ever happen again. Keats's verse has been harvested and gleaned very thoroughly.

It is useless to praise him here, and to limit his achievement critically is not a matter of consequence so long as his poems enchant and inspire. The reflection even that he could not advance 'the way that he was going' when in the second version of *Hyperion* he spoke of the difference between the poet and the dreamer—the knowledge that crass casualty broke in and stopped him just when he knew the road ahead—does not alter the actual situation. Keats knew himself that 'the height' is attained from something else besides appreciations of loveliness and bliss, but he also discerned that a certain simplicity is the final magic.

His friends, with some exceptions, cultivated him with vague praise, as though they were raising the most scented, gorgeous show-rose ever exhibited. He was too young to challenge them on their tastes and objects, until it did not matter much to him. But again this is not a burning question now. He was very near a defiant simplicity in the 'Ode to a Grecian Urn'. The Urn may have been anything but Grecian; but the faith 'Beauty is truth', or as some would rather say the philosophy, stands undisturbed, and the manner is purified into an almost Flaxmanesque modesty.

Among the most candid and praiseworthy things ever said by Keats of himself, however intrusively it takes its place in its original setting, this is one:

> For I would not be dieted with praise,
> A pet-lamb in a sentimental farce.

It is by the way of a farewell to Love, Ambition, and Poesy, towards the end of the 'Ode on Indolence'. It goes beyond the poem, and is always applicable. Keats perceived that, though poets love praise, they cannot and they would not escape from the 'secret battle' which is fought between them and certain dark angels.

At the moment, 'Keats Museums' are found in his old Hampstead headquarters, in the Piazza di Spagna in Rome, at Harvard University, and probably elsewhere. The number of locks of hair from the poet's red-gold poll seems to increase. The least detail of his correspondence is apt to set going one of those opposites to pen-friendship over which weary literary editors at last write the formula, 'This correspondence must now cease'. And all this is in its way delightful and humane; yet it is not quite what Keats was looking for, nor what poetry is about.

It was only by degrees that Keats himself apprehended what poetry is about. He sprang to it with shining ease when he did; but he was too long instructed, even by his kindest mentors, that it was a paradise of dainty devices. These are not to be despised, but he noted even at the outset that the poetry of things as they are was a possibility and a kind of duty for himself, and in the revision of *Hyperion* he saw that much better. That was the essence. Even then he could not exchange his general habit either of method or metre for a great freedom, of which he perceived the glory. And from that hour his time was short.

Where shall we rank him? Is he in his own way a Mendelssohn, a Theocritus, a Corot, a junior Shakespeare? The answer rests with his readers, and the documents on which they must base it are many, lovely, and inviting. It is the experience of the writer of these pages that to a number of men and women Keats is without parallel; to them, through all that he wrote and all that was written upon him, through all his portraits and whatever is now known to have been his in any degree, he is as Mrs Browning isolated him in *Aurora Leigh* more than a century ago,

The man who never stepped
In gradual progress like another man,
But, turning grandly on his central self,
Ensphered himself in twenty perfect years
And died, not young—(the life of a long life
Distilled to a mere drop, falling like a tear
Upon the world's cold cheek, to make it burn
For ever).

# JOHN KEATS
## A Select Bibliography

(Place of publication London, unless stated otherwise. Detailed biblio-graphical information will also be found in the appropriate volumes of *The Cambridge Bibliography of English Literature* and *The Oxford History of English Literature*).

*Bibliography:*

CATALOGUE OF A LOAN EXHIBITION Commemorating the Anniversary of the Death of John Keats (1821–1921) held at the Public Library, Boston, February 21–March 14, 1921.

THE JOHN KEATS MEMORIAL VOLUME (1921)
—contains 'A Bibliography of the Writings of John Keats', by T. J. Wise.

THE ASHLEY LIBRARY. A Catalogue of Printed Books, Manuscripts and Letters collected by T. J. Wise (1928)
—printed for private circulation. Contains a description of books and MSS by or relating to Keats.

KEATS. A Bibliography and reference guide, with an essay on Keats's reputation, by J. R. Macgillivray (1949).

KEATS, SHELLEY, BYRON, HUNT AND THEIR CIRCLES. A Bibliography July 1, 1950–June 30, 1962, ed. D. Bonnell Green and E. G. Wilson; Nebraska, 1964.

*Collected Editions*

THE POETICAL WORKS OF COLERIDGE, SHELLEY AND KEATS; Paris (1829)
—the Galignani edition.

THE POETICAL WORKS (1840)
—in Smith's Standard Library. The first English collected edition.

THE POETICAL WORKS. With a Memoir by R. M. Milnes [Lord Houghton] (1854)
—the first illustrated edition, with 120 designs by George Scharf.

THE POETICAL WORKS, ed., with a Critical Memoir by W. M. Rossetti (1872).

THE POETICAL WORKS, ed. Lord Houghton [R. M. Milnes] (1876)
—the Aldine Edition.

THE POETICAL WORKS AND OTHER WRITINGS, ed. H. Buxton Forman. 4 vols (1883)
—Vols. III and IV contain Keats's letters.

THE POEMS, ed. G. Thorn-Drury. With an introduction by R. Bridges, 2 vols (1896).

THE COMPLETE POETICAL WORKS AND LETTERS, ed. H. E. Scudder; Boston and New York (1899)
—the Cambridge Edition.

THE COMPLETE WORKS, ed. H. Buxton Forman, 5 vols; Glasgow (1900–1)
—brings the editions of 1883 and 1889 up to date with new material and biographical notes.

THE POEMS, ed. E. de Selincourt (1905)
—with authoritative introduction and notes. Rev. editions, 1907 and 1926.

THE POETICAL WORKS, ed. H. Buxton Forman (1906). With Introduction and textual notes; ed. H. W. Garrod, 1956.

POEMS OF JOHN KEATS, ed. and arranged in chronological order by J. M. Murry (1930).

POETICAL WORKS, ed. H. W. Garrod (1939)
—the Oxford Variorium edition, revised 1958.


*Selected Works:*

THE EVE OF ST AGNES AND OTHER POEMS; Boston (1876)
—part of the 'Vest-Pocket' Series of Standard and Popular Authors.

ODES AND SONNETS; Philadelphia (1888)
—with illustrative designs by W. H. Low.

SELECTIONS FROM KEATS (1889)
—with a preface by J. R. Tutin. Includes all the poems from the 1820 volume and a selection from the other.

THE ODES OF KEATS, with Notes and Analyses and a Memoir by A. C. Downer (1897)
—facsimile of 1897 edition, Tokyo, 1965.

ENDYMION AND THE LONGER POEMS, ed. H. Buxton Forman (1897).

POETRY AND PROSE, ed. H. Ellershaw (1922)
—with essays by Lamb, Leigh Hunt, Bridges.

POEMS. With Selections from his Letters and from Criticism, ed. G. W. Thomas (1932)
—includes criticism by de Selincourt, Bridges, Bradley.

SELECTED LETTERS AND POEMS, ed. J. A. Walsh (1954).

SELECTED POEMS, ed. E. C. Blunden (1955).

SELECTED POEMS AND LETTERS OF JOHN KEATS, ed. R. Gittings (1967).

*Separate Works:*

POEMS (1817)
—a facsimile of the 1817 edition in the Noel Douglas Replicas series, 1927.

ENDYMION: A POETIC ROMANCE (1818)
—a type-facsimile edition with introduction and notes by C. E. Notcutt, 1927. See also T. Saito's edition of *Endymion*, with notes, 1931.

LAMIA, ISABELLA, THE EVE OF ST AGNES, AND OTHER POEMS (1820).

ANOTHER VERSION OF KEATS'S HYPERION [1857?]
—reprint of R. M. Milnes' contribution to the *Miscellanies of the Philobiblon Society*, III, 1856–7. The basic text of *The Fall of Hyperion: A Dream* until the discovery of the Woodhouse Transcript in 1904.

'La Belle Dame Sans Merci', *The Indicator*, 10 May, 1820
—the poem is signed 'Caviare'.

HYPERION. A Facsimile of Keats's Autograph Manuscript with a Transliteration of the Manuscript of *The Fall of Hyperion: A Dream*, with Introduction and Notes by E. de Selincourt (1905).

*Note:* Students should also consult *The Examiner, The Indicator, The Annals of the Fine Arts, Blackwood's Magazine* and other journals of Keats's day.


*Letters:*

LETTERS TO FANNY BRAWNE, 1819–1820. With Introduction and Notes by H. Buxton Forman (1878).

LETTERS, ed. J. G. Speed; New York (1883).

LETTERS TO HIS FAMILY AND FRIENDS, ed. S. Colvin (1891)
—excludes letters to Fanny Brawne.

LETTERS, ed. H. Buxton Forman (1895)
—contains every letter of Keats known at the time.

THE KEATS LETTERS, PAPERS AND OTHER RELICS FORMING THE DILKE BEQUEST, ed. T. Watts-Dunton, G. Williamson and H. Buxton Forman (1914).

LETTERS, ed. M. B. Forman, 2 vols (1931)
—the definitive edition. The revised edition of 1935 adds ten further letters. Ed. H. E. Rollins, 1958.

AUTOBIOGRAPHY OF JOHN KEATS, COMPILED FROM HIS LETTERS AND ESSAYS, ed. E. V. Weller; Palo Alto (1933).

THE KEATS CIRCLE: LETTERS AND PAPERS 1816–78, ed. H. E. Rollins. 2 vols; Cambridge, Mass. (1948).

MORE LETTERS AND POEMS OF THE KEATS CIRCLE, ed. H. E. Rollins; Cambridge, Mass. (1955)

—a new edition entitled *The Keats Circle: Letters and Papers and More Letters and Poems of the Keats Circle*, 1965, contains the 1948 and 1955 publications in 2 vols.

*Note:* See also *Collected Editions, Selected Works* and *Some Biographical and Critical Studies.*

*Some Biographical and Critical Studies:*

ADONAIS: AN ELEGY ON THE DEATH OF JOHN KEATS, by P. B. Shelley, 1821.

LORD BYRON AND SOME OF HIS CONTEMPORARIES, by L. Hunt (1828)

—contains an account of Keats with criticism of his poetry. Ed. J. E. Morpurgo, 1949.

THE BOOK OF GEMS, Vol. III, ed. S. C. Hall (1838)

—contains comment on Keats by L. Hunt.

IMAGINATION AND FANCY, by L. Hunt (1844)

—ed. Sir E. Gosse, 1907.

THE LIFE OF PERCY BYSSHE SHELLEY, by T. Medwin, 2 vols (1847)

—contains comment on Keats, based on information from Leigh Hunt, Fanny Brawne and Shelley.

LIFE, LETTERS AND LITERARY REMAINS OF JOHN KEATS, by R. M. Milnes [Lord Houghton], 2 vols, (1948)

—contains many poems not previously published including Keats's tragedy, *Otho the Great.*

POETICS: AN ESSAY ON POETRY, by E. S. Dallas (1852).

LIFE OF B. R. HAYDON FROM HIS AUTOBIOGRAPHY AND JOURNALS, ed. T. Taylor, 3 vols (1853).

ON THE STUDY OF CELTIC LITERATURE, by M. Arnold (1867).

MY STUDY WINDOWS, ed. J. R. Lowell (1871)

—forming part of Low's American Copyright Series of American Authors.

THE PAPERS OF A CRITIC, by Sir C. W. Dilke, 2 vols (1875)

—the Memoir by Sir C. W. Dilke contains letters from Keats, etc.

RECOLLECTIONS OF WRITERS, by C. and M. Cowden Clarke (1878).

THE ENGLISH POETS. SELECTIONS, with a general introduction by M. Arnold, ed. T. H. Ward (1880)

—Vol IV contains essay on Keats by M. Arnold, republished in *Essays in Criticism*, 1888.

JOHN KEATS, A STUDY, by F. M. Owen (1880).

KEATS, by S. Colvin (1887)
—in the *English Men of Letters* Series. New edition, 1889.

LIFE OF JOHN KEATS, by W. M. Rossetti (1887)
—contains a bibliography by J. P. Anderson.

THE LIFE AND LETTERS OF JOSEPH SEVERN, by W. Sharp (1892).

JOHN KEATS, A CRITICAL ESSAY, by R. Bridges (1895)
—privately printed; published in the Muses' Library, 1896. Republished in *Collected Essays*, IV. 1929.

*The Bookman.* Keats Double Number, October 1906
—contains original material relating to Keats.

OXFORD LECTURES ON POETRY, by A. C. Bradley (1909)
—contains an essay on 'The Letters of Keats'.

JOHN KEATS: SA VIE ET SON OEUVRE, 1795–1821, by L. Wolff; Paris (1910).

KEATS, by E. Thomas (1916).

A CONCORDANCE TO THE POEMS OF JOHN KEATS, ed. D. L. Baldwin; Washington (1917).

JOHN KEATS: HIS LIFE AND POETRY, HIS FRIENDS, CRITICS AND AFTER-FAME, by S. Colvin (1917).
—rev. edition, 1925.

JOHN KEATS MEMORIAL VOLUME, issued by Keats House Committee, Hampstead (1921).

KEATS, A STUDY IN DEVELOPMENT, by H. I'A. Fausset (1922).

JOHN KEATS, by A. Lowell, 2 vols; Boston (1925).

KEATS AND SHAKESPEARE. A Study of Keats's Poetic Life from 1816 to 1820, by J. M. Murry (1925).

KEATS, by H. W. Garrod (1926).

THE LIFE AND LETTERS OF JOHN KEATS, by Lord Houghton (1927).

KEATS'S SHAKESPEARE: A DESCRIPTIVE STUDY, by C. Spurgeon (1928).

JOHN HAMILTON REYNOLDS, POETRY AND PROSE, with an Introduction and Notes by G. L. Marsh (1928).

KEATS'S VIEW OF POETRY, by T. Saito (1929).

KEATS, by L. Wolff; Paris (1929).

KEATS'S CRAFTSMANSHIP. A Study in Poetic Development, by M. R. Ridley; Oxford (1933).

KEATS HOUSE AND MUSEUM: An Historical and Descriptive Guide (1934)
—new edition 1966.

KEATS'S PUBLISHER: A MEMOIR OF JOHN TAYLOR, by E. Blunden (1936).

THE EVOLUTION OF KEATS'S POETRY, by C. L. Finney; Cambridge, Mass. (1936).

JOHN KEATS, by T. Saito; Tokyo (1936)

—text in Japanese.

LIFE OF JOHN KEATS, by C. A. Brown (1937), ed. with an Introduction and notes by D. H. Bodurtha and W. B. Pope (1937).

ADONAIS: A LIFE OF JOHN KEATS, by D. Hewlett (1937)

—revised and enlarged edition, entitled *A Life of Keats*, 1949.

KEATS AS DOCTOR AND PATIENT, by W. H. White; Oxford (1938).

ROMANTIC POETRY AND THE FINE ARTS, by E. Blunden (1942).

KEATS, SHELLEY AND ROME. Compiled by N. Rogers (1949).

THE OPPOSING SELF: NINE ESSAYS IN CRITICISM by L. Trilling; New York (1950)

—contains 'The Poet as a Hero', 'Keats in His Letters'.

FANNY BRAWNE, by J. Richardson (1952).

JOHN KEATS: THE LIVING YEAR, 1818–1819 by R. Gittings (1954).

KEATS, by J. M. Murry (1955)

—incorporates *Studies in Keats*, 1930 (1939) and *The Mystery of Keats*, 1949.

THE MASK OF KEATS: A Study of Problems, by R. Gittings (1956).

ON THE POETRY OF KEATS, by E. C. Pettet (1957).

JOHN KEATS: A REASSESSMENT, ed. K. Muir; Liverpool (1958).

THE CONSECRATED URN: An Interpretation of Keats in Growth and Form, by B. Blackstone (1959).

JOHN KEATS, by W. J. Bate; Cambridge, Mass. (1963).

THE EVERLASTING SPELL, by J. Richardson (1963).

JOHN KEATS: THE MAKING OF A POET, by A. Ward (1963).

THE KEATS INHERITANCE, by R. Gittings (1964).

AESTHETIC AND MYTH IN THE POETRY OF KEATS, by W. H. Evert (1965).

KEATS AND THE MIRROR OF ART, by I. Jack (1967)

—an examination of Keats's cultural milieu, especially the influence of painters and art critics on his poetic development.

CRITICS ON KEATS, ed. J. O'Neill (1967)

—selections from important critical works arranged in chronological order of Keats's writings.

JOHN KEATS, by R. Gittings (1968).

*Note:* The Bulletin of the Keats-Shelley Memorial, Rome (I, 1910; II, 1913, ed. Sir R. Rodd and H. N. Gay, republished 1962; III [etc.] ed. D. Hewlett, 1950–    ) contains much valuable information not available elsewhere.

# WRITERS AND THEIR WORK

CLOUGH: Isobel Armstrong
COLERIDGE: Kathleen Raine
CREEVEY & GREVILLE: J. Richardson
DE QUINCEY: Hugh Sykes Davies
DICKENS: K. J. Fielding
   EARLY NOVELS: T. Blount
   LATER NOVELS: B. Hardy
DISRAELI: Paul Bloomfield
GEORGE ELIOT: Lettice Cooper
FERRIER & GALT: W. M. Parker
FITZGERALD: Joanna Richardson
MRS. GASKELL: Miriam Allott
GISSING: A. C. Ward
THOMAS HARDY: R. A. Scott-James
      and C. Day Lewis
HAZLITT: J. B. Priestley
HOOD: Laurence Brander
G. M. HOPKINS: Geoffrey Grigson
T. H. HUXLEY: William Irvine
KEATS: Edmund Blunden
LAMB: Edmund Blunden
LANDOR: G. Rostrevor Hamilton
EDWARD LEAR: Joanna Richardson
MACAULAY: G. R. Potter
MEREDITH: Phyllis Bartlett
JOHN STUART MILL: M. Cranston
WILLIAM MORRIS: P. Henderson
NEWMAN: J. M. Cameron
PATER: Iain Fletcher
PEACOCK: J. I. M. Stewart
ROSSETTI: Oswald Doughty
CHRISTINA ROSSETTI: G. Battiscombe
RUSKIN: Peter Quennell
SIR WALTER SCOTT: Ian Jack
SHELLEY: Stephen Spender
SOUTHEY: Geoffrey Carnall
R. L. STEVENSON: G. B. Stern
SWINBURNE: H. J. C. Grierson
TENNYSON: F. L. Lucas
THACKERAY: Laurence Brander
FRANCIS THOMPSON: P. Butter
TROLLOPE: Hugh Sykes Davies
OSCAR WILDE: James Laver
WORDSWORTH: Helen Darbishire

*Twentieth Century:*
CHINUA ACHEBE: A. Ravenscroft
W. H. AUDEN: Richard Hoggart
HILAIRE BELLOC: Renée Haynes
ARNOLD BENNETT: F. Swinnerton
EDMUND BLUNDEN: Alec M. Hardie
ELIZABETH BOWEN: Jocelyn Brooke
ROBERT BRIDGES: J. Sparrow
ROY CAMPBELL: David Wright
JOYCE CARY: Walter Allen
G. K. CHESTERTON: C. Hollis
WINSTON CHURCHILL: John Connell
R. G. COLLINGWOOD: E.W.F. Tomlin

I. COMPTON-BURNETT: P. H. Johnson
JOSEPH CONRAD: Oliver Warner
WALTER DE LA MARE: K. Hopkins
NORMAN DOUGLAS: Ian Greenlees
T. S. ELIOT: M. C. Bradbrook
FIRBANK & BETJEMAN: J. Brooke
FORD MADOX FORD: Kenneth Young
E. M. FORSTER: Rex Warner
CHRISTOPHER FRY: Derek Stanford
JOHN GALSWORTHY: R. H. Mottram
WM GOLDING: Clive Pemberton
ROBERT GRAVES: M. Seymour-Smith
GRAHAM GREENE: Francis Wyndham
L. P. HARTLEY & ANTHONY POWELL:
      P. Bloomfield and B. Bergonzi
A. E. HOUSMAN: Ian Scott-Kilvert
ALDOUS HUXLEY: Jocelyn Brooke
HENRY JAMES: Michael Swan
PAMELA HANSFORD JOHNSON:
           Isabel Quigly
JAMES JOYCE: J. I. M. Stewart
RUDYARD KIPLING: Bonamy Dobree
D. H. LAWRENCE: Kenneth Young
C. DAY LEWIS: Clifford Dyment
WYNDHAM LEWIS: E. W. F. Tomlin
COMPTON MACKENZIE: K. Young
LOUIS MACNEICE: John Press
KATHERINE MANSFIELD: Ian Gordon
JOHN MASEFIELD: L. A. G. Strong
SOMERSET MAUGHAM: J. Brophy
GEORGE MOORE: A. Norman Jeffares
J. MIDDLETON MURRY: Philip Mairet
SEAN O'CASEY: W. A. Armstrong
GEORGE ORWELL: Tom Hopkinson
JOHN OSBORNE: Simon Trussler
HAROLD PINTER: J. R. Taylor
POETS OF 1939-45 WAR: R. N. Currey
POWYS BROTHERS: R. C. Churchill
J. B. PRIESTLEY: Ivor Brown
HERBERT READ: Francis Berry
FOUR REALIST NOVELISTS: V. Brome
BERNARD SHAW: A. C. Ward
EDITH SITWELL: John Lehmann
OSBERT SITWELL: Roger Fulford
KENNETH SLESSOR: C. Semmler
C. P. SNOW: William Cooper
SYNGE & LADY GREGORY: E. Coxhead
DYLAN THOMAS: G. S. Fraser
G. M. TREVELYAN: J. H. Plumb
WAR POETS: 1914-18: E. Blunden
EVELYN WAUGH: Christopher Hollis
H. G. WELLS: Montgomery Belgion
PATRICK WHITE: R. F. Brissenden
ANGUS WILSON: K. W. Gransden
VIRGINIA WOOLF: B. Blackstone
W. B. YEATS: G. S. Fraser
ANDREW YOUNG & R. S. THOMAS:
      L. Clark and R. G. Thomas